CENGAGE Learning

Novels for Students, Volume 2

Copyright © 1997

Gale Research
835 Penobscot Building
645 Griswold St.
Detroit, Ml 48226-4094

ISBN 0-7876-1687-7
ISSN 1094-3552

Printed in the United States of America
10 9 8 7 6 5 4

I Know Why the Caged Bird Sings

Maya Angelou

1970

Introduction

I Know Why the Caged Bird Sings is the first—and many say the best—of five autobiographical volumes the gifted African American author, Maya Angelou, wrote. It is a remarkably vivid retelling of the turbulent events of her childhood, during which she shuttled back and forth between dramatically different environments in rural Stamps, Arkansas, slightly raunchy St. Louis, Missouri, and glitzy San Francisco, California. It is also the annals of her relationships with a rich and diverse cast of characters. Chief among these are her determined, strict, and wise grandmother Annie Henderson; her crippled and bitter uncle Willie Johnson; her bright and imaginative brother Bailey Johnson Jr.; her playboy father Bailey Johnson; and her beautiful, brilliant, and worldly mother, Vivian Baxter Johnson. A host of other unforgettable characters fill out the cast for this earnest, sometimes sardonic retelling of the drama of Maya Angelou's growing-up years. During these years, she struggled against the odds of being black at a time when prejudice, especially in the South, was at its height. But most of all her story is the story of discovering who she is —of working her way through a multifaceted identity crisis. The source of the title of the book is a poem by Paul Laurence Dunbar entitled "Sympathy." "I know why the caged bird sings," writes the poet. "When he beats his bars and he would be free. It is a plea, that upward to Heaven he flings. I know why the caged bird sings!"

When Maya Angelou was three and her brother, Bailey, was four, her parents divorced and shipped the two young children to live with their paternal grandmother, Annie Henderson, in the stark, dusty black section of Stamps, Arkansas. Annie had status in the black community: She owned and ran a successful general store that supplied the black community with food and sundries. She also owned an extra house that she rented to a family of poor white people who occasionally came to the store to taunt her and her family.

During the Depression, Mrs. Johnson (also known as Sister Johnson) was able to lend money to both blacks and whites in need of cash. Later, she was able to use this as a kind of clout when she confronted offensive former borrowers. Stolid, confident, strong and wise, she was Maya and Bailey's first role model—a strict one who taught them cleanliness, godliness, and respect for others. Their lives revolved around the store and its customers and the church, which Maya viewed with a certain amount of skepticism.

A bright child, as was her brother, she learned quickly and did well in the black school she attended. An elegant neighbor, Mrs. Flowers, took Maya under her wing and taught her to love books. The children adjusted well to life in Stamps, in spite of the prejudice they experienced from and toward whites. Their lives were rich with people, including grumpy Uncle Willie, their crippled uncle who hung out in the store most of the time, unable to do any meaningful work. They were part of a close, caring community that extended to the bridge that transversed the gap that sharply divided the black and white sections of town.

Suddenly one day, the children's father, Bailey Johnson Sr., arrived in a car to swoop them up and take them to live with their mother, Vivian Baxter Johnson, in St. Louis. Through good looks, wits and guts, their mother was able to provide them with a better standard of living. But disaster struck when their mother's live-in boyfriend, Mr. Freeman, seduced and violently raped Maya. After a brief court trial, Freeman was sentenced to jail. He never made it: their mother's brothers beat him to death behind a slaughter house. Hospitalized for her injuries and traumatized, Maya returned home a changed child. She would not talk or smile. To others, she was thoroughly disagreeable. Finally, her mother was unable to tolerate this behavior any longer. She returned the children to their grandmother in Stamps, where Maya gradually came out of her shell and resumed the familiar patterns of her pre-St. Louis life.

After graduating from grade school, she and her brother returned to live with their mother, who had moved to San Francisco. With her mother's support, Maya became a confident teenager who managed to force her way into a job as a streetcar conductor at the age of fifteen. She was the first black to achieve this status. Confused about her sexuality, she decided to prove she was a normal woman by demanding and having sex with a young neighbor. The one-time liaison ended up with the birth of Maya's son, Guy Johnson.

As she continued her journey toward adulthood and ultimate multiple successes, she experienced life at its best and at its worst. At one point, she brushed against prostitution and drugs. Her several marriages ended in divorce, in part because she had so many agendas for her life. She kept her first husband's name as her surname. After completing high school in San Francisco and attending an art school there, she studied music and dance, tutored in the latter art with dancers Martha Graham, Pearl Primus and Ann Halprin. She also studied drama with Frank Silvera and Gene Frankel. She became a dancer, playwright, actress, director, singer, poet, composer and politician. She spent four years in Ghana pursuing a knowledge of her heritage—and discovered that essentially she was an American. Tapped by Martin Luther King, she served as Northern coordinator of the Southern Christian Leadership Converence in 1959 and 1960, and published the first of her series of autobiographical novels, *I Know Why the Caged Bird Sings,* in 1970. She has been a writer in residence and a professor at numerous universities around the world, won numerous awards for both acting and writing and received honorary degrees from leading universities and served on the boards of several prestigious arts and civic organizations.

She was honored at President Clinton's first inauguration in 1993, where she recited one of her celebrated poems.

Plot Summary

Part I

The first of five autobiographical works, *I Know Why the Caged Bird Sings,* focuses on the recollections and adult understanding of Maya Angelou's growing up female and black in the America of the 1930s and 1940s. The author begins this volume with a description of her young self standing in front of the church to deliver a short poem on Easter. Although she describes herself as very dark and ugly with "steel wool" for hair, here she imagines that someday her true self will emerge. She'll be blonde, blue-eyed, and white.

The first chapter proper, however, shows us three-year-old Marguerite (Maya) and her four-year-old brother Bailey arriving by train to live with their father's mother, Mrs. Annie Henderson, in Stamps, Arkansas. The children's parents have ended their marriage and sent the young children off by train with notes instructing "To Whom It May Concern" of their names, origin, and destination. Once in Stamps, the children's lives revolve around the church, the school, and helping "Momma" and their lame Uncle Willie with the Wm. Johnson General Merchandise Store, referred to by all in the community as "The Store." Their grandmother had built the business up from a simple lunch wagon for field workers.

Since the Store acts as a focus of the community, Marguerite and Bailey become acquainted with the daily lives of everyone in the black section of town. They wait on the field hands before they load up in wagons reminiscent of the plantations and serve them in the evenings when they return worn and beaten from the fields. They know Mr. McElroy as an independent black man. They watch the Reverend H. Thomas get the best of the Sunday chicken. And they survive the Depression and keep the Store going by exchanging commodities given out by the government for items from the shelves. The children do their lessons under Uncle Willie's stern hand and fall in love with books, especially Shakespeare, around the fire in the back of the store at night.

Part II—St. Louis

Quite suddenly, though, their father shows up in Stamps with no prior contact but Christmas presents the year before. Their father drives Marguerite and Bailey to their mother and her family in St. Louis. Here, Grandmother Baxter presides as a Precinct Captain, and their loud, tough uncles have city jobs. Their mother, Vivian Baxter, whom Bailey names "Mother Dear," has been trained as a pediatric nurse but lives with Mr. Freeman and supplements her income by dealing cards. Marguerite and Bailey adjust quickly to city life and do well in school.

One morning when Mother hasn't come home

yet and Bailey is out, Mr. Freeman approaches Marguerite sexually. She had sat on his lap and hugged him before, mistaking his attentions as ordinary and "fatherly." Today, however, he turns up the volume on the radio to drown out her cries and brutally rapes the eight-year-old girl. When he is finished, he warns her that if she tells, he'll kill Bailey.

> "We were just playing before." He released me enough to snatch down my bloomers, and then he dragged me closer to him. Turning the radio up loud, too loud, he said, 'if you scream, I'm gonna kill you. And if you tell, I'm gonna kill Bailey.' I could tell he meant what he said. I couldn't understand why he wanted to kill my brother. Neither of us had done anything to him. And then.

> Then there was the pain. A breaking and entering when even the senses are torn apart. The act of rape on an eight-year-old body is a matter of the needle giving because the camel can't. The child gives, because the body can, and the mind of the violator cannot.

Unable to hide the injury from Maya's mother, Mr. Freeman is discovered, and he is put on trial for the crime. When his lawyer gets him freed on a technicality, his body is later found. Presumably, the uncles have kicked him to death. At this point

Marguerite feels responsible for his death and stops talking. Without explanation, the children soon find themselves on a train going back to Stamps. Their lives resume as before they left, with the community accepting them completely.

Part III—Return to Stamps

Back in the rural South, Marguerite witnesses her grandmother's triumph when some young white girls try to shame her. Joe Louis keeps the World's Heavy-Weight Championship title while they listen on the store's radio. After years of silence, Marguerite is befriended by Mrs. Bertha Flowers, a "gentlewoman" who gently persuades her to begin talking again by loaning her books to be read aloud and together. At a picnic Marguerite sneaks off to read and then makes her first friend of her own age. She graduates with honors from grammar school in 1940. She works for a short while as domestic help.

Momma abruptly decides to take them to their parents, who now live in California, when Bailey comes to the Store in shock. He had been made to handle a dead black man's body and witness the brutality of whites to blacks. Bailey cannot understand the hatred, and his grandmother fears for his safety.

Part IV—California

World War II has just started, and San Francisco booms with wartime activities. Their mother is now married to "Daddy Clidell," the first father Marguerite knows. She attends a nearly all-white school and does well, but is bored except for social studies and night classes she takes at the California Labor School. Marguerite has many glamorous day-dreams when her father invites her "to vacation" with him in southern California. Once there, however, she becomes quickly disillusioned with her father's girlfriend, the trailer park, and her father.

On a day trip to Mexico with her father, she gets a glimpse of the exotic life she had imagined. But her father gets too drunk, and Marguerite drives them all the way to the border, nearly without mishap. Back at the trailer, her father's girlfriend Dolores cuts Marguerite during a fight. Her father takes Marguerite to friends, but she leaves and finds herself part of a racially mixed community of young people living on their own in a junkyard. After a month, she calls her mother and returns to San Francisco.

In San Francisco she finds her brother and mother constantly at odds until Bailey finally moves out, eventually joining the Merchant Marines. Dissatisfied and restless, Marguerite decides to get a job. She ends up battling bureaucracy to become the first black conductorette on the street cars. Still young, but more mature than her peers, Marguerite becomes confused by her newly awakening sexual feelings and seduces a young man.

Three weeks later she realizes she's pregnant, but on Bailey's advice keeps the pregnancy a secret so that she can finish high school. Once she has graduated two days after V-Day, she leaves a note on Daddy Clidell's bed informing her parents of her pregnancy. Soon after, her son is born, and her mother takes care of him. Maya loves her son, but is afraid to touch him because she's always been "awkward." Finally, however, her mother puts the three-week old baby to sleep with Marguerite. At first Marguerite protests, then struggles to say awake so she won't crush the baby. Later on, though, her mother wakes her to demonstrate how she has protected her son even in her sleep.

Characters

Vivian Baxter Bailey

Maya's mother is a beautiful, sexy, vibrant, smart woman with more than a little common sense. She loves her children, and she listens to them uncritically—with the exception of her final blow-up with Bailey Jr. Energetic, she pursues several careers. She rents out rooms in her large home in San Francisco and manages casinos. She is also a one-time nurse. She gradually weans Maya from the restricted environment of Stamps and brings her into the freer environment of a city without lynchings. She's not afraid to confront people who have displeased her. For example, when she learns that Mr. Freeman has raped Maya, he's out the door immediately. She carries a gun and uses it strategically when she is threatened by a traitorous business partner. A strong and appealing individual, she is unforgettable.

Grandmother Baxter

Grandmother Baxter, Maya's maternal grandmother, was an octoroon—a person with one-eighth African American blood—which meant that her skin was white. She plays a very minor role in Maya's life, but she's interesting because she has infiltrated St. Louis politics to the point where she has considerable influence.

Daddy Clidell

Daddy Clidell, Mother's second husband, is "the first father I would know." A successful businessman, he adds stability to Maya's life.

Daddy

See Bailey Johnson Sr.

Mrs. Flowers

Mrs. Flowers is an elegant black lady who lives in Stamps. She makes Maya proud to be an African American. Knowing that Maya is an outstanding student, she provides her with the best of literature and introduces her to formal customs such as afternoon tea.

Mrs. Annie Henderson

Maya's grandmother, whom Maya calls Momma, is a strong, independent, righteous woman. Her family, her store, and her church are the focal points of her life. She rules Maya and Bailey with an iron hand and a velvet glove, teaching them cleanliness, godliness, respect, and courtesy. Successful and prosperous, she is never stingy. During the Depression, she lends money to blacks and whites alike. Later she takes her chances by taking a dangerously ill Maya to a white dentist. When he refuses to treat a Negro, she tells him to get out of town that very day. He is rightfully intimidated by her. She is a strong, determined, and unafraid woman. Nevertheless, she knows the boundaries of the prejudiced society in which the black people of Stamps dwell. The threat of a lynching is never far away. Says Maya of her grandmother, "I don't think she ever knew that a deep-brooding love hung over everything she touched."

Media Adaptations

- *Know Why the Caged Bird Sings* was made into a TV movie in 1979 starring Diahann Carroll, Ruby Dee, Esther Rolle, Roger E. Mosely, Paul Benjamin, and Constance Good, directed by Fielder Cook. Available from Knowledge Unlimited, Inc.

Bailey Johnson Jr.

Maya's brother, Bailey, is her best friend. A bright and imaginative companion, he shares her love of books and of drama. Bailey is somewhat more likely than Maya to get into trouble (but nothing major), especially when he reaches his adolescent years. He has a brief sexual affair with a rather loose girl. He loves St. Louis and his mother and resents it when he has to return to Stamps because of Maya's withdrawal after the rape. When he is sixteen, he moves out of his mother's San Francisco house after he and his mother have a fight. Basically, they can't live with each other and they can't live without each other, Maya explains. Eventually, Bailey joins the Merchant Marine.

Bailey Johnson Sr.

Maya's unpredictable father, Bailey Johnson Sr., cares about his children but only in a casual way. Well spoken and impeccably dressed, he earns his living as a doorman in a hotel. Before that, he was a dietician in the U.S. Navy. But at heart he's a boastful, self-important, hard-drinking playboy who sleeps around and deceives women about his marital intentions.

Marguerite Johnson

See Maya Johnson

Maya Johnson

Maya Johnson is a brilliant, sensitive young black woman with keen insight into her environment and the people in it. Her observations and her expressed feelings are so real that the reader begins to absorb her vivid if tragic universe. Early on in the book, she describes herself as "a too-big Negro girl, with nappy black hair, broad feet and a space between her teeth that would hold a number-two pencil." Her childhood dream is to wake up some day with light-blue eyes and long, straight blond hair.

Life in Stamps is timeless but not tedious. The days and seasons follow one another in orderly sequence as Maya helps in the store, attends school, play-acts with her brother Bailey Jr., listens to grown-up talk as neighbors gather in the store and attends church services and church picnics (the latter usually with a sense of skeptical irony). Maya's mentor, the elegant Mrs. Flowers, introduces her to the world of literature and afternoon tea.

Mischief as well as irony is very much part of Maya's nature. When she takes a job as a maid in a white person's house, her employer's friends urge them to call her Mary, not Marguerite, deeming the latter too long a name for a little black girl. She manages to extricate herself from the unpleasant situation by plotting with Bailey to break her employer's favorite piece of bric-a-brac. Solitary and within herself, teased by schoolmates, Maya has few friends her own age, although she finally links up with another school pariah, Louise Kendricks.

The sudden departure from Stamps to St. Louis is traumatic at first. But when Maya meets her beautiful, lively, smart mother, she likes her immediately. It is a different world in St. Louis— one where her mother prospers by pursuing several careers—as a realtor, an entertainer, and a casino hostess. All would have been fine if Mr. Freeman, her mother's boyfriend, had not raped her. But after the hospitalization, the trial, and the trauma, Maya becomes a gloomy and silent child. Soon, her mother sends both Maya and Bailey back to Stamps and their grandmother. Maya seems to shift from one environment to the other automatically. Her adaptability and acceptance of change is amazing— as is her growing independence, which may be the inevitable result of never knowing where She'll be next.

Back in San Francisco with her mother, after an abortive Mexican vacation with her father and a one-month stay with homeless kids in Los Angeles, she begins to acquire self-confidence. At the age of fifteen, she lies her way into a job as a streetcar conductor—the first black conductor ever hired. Confused by her emerging sexuality, she decides to prove that she is a woman by inviting a teenage neighbor to have sex with her. This one-time encounter results in pregnancy. With a teenager's characteristic avoidance of unpleasant confrontations, she keeps the pending birth to herself until three weeks before the baby is born.

Finally, she takes the baby boy into her bed and heart—with the encouragement of her mother.

Miss Kirwin

Miss Kirwin is Maya's favorite teacher at San Francisco's George Washington High School, which Maya describes as "the first real school I attended." Miss Kirwin is one of those rare teachers who respect their students. She is also able to stimulate their minds by getting them involved in the *San Francisco Chronicle* and other news media.

Momma

See Annie Henderson

Mother

See Vivian Baxter Bailey

Ritie

See Maya Johnson

Sister

See Annie Henderson

George Taylor

A self-pitying Stamps widower who uses his grief as a way to win the sympathy of others.

Ignorant and superstitious, he frightens the young Maya by saying that he saw a blue-eyed baby angel hovering over him.

The Reverend Howard Thomas

A pompous preacher who makes the circuit of the Arkansas area that includes Stamps. He visits every three months and stays with the Johnsons. A colossal eater, he is fat and slovenly. Maya and Bailey hate him.

Uncle Willie

Maya's Uncle Willie is a proud but shattered man. Rendered a cripple by some childhood accident, he desperately seeks a way to be needed and appreciated. When some strangers come to buy something, he pulls himself up erect behind the counter and pretends to be normal—probably enduring great pain in the process. While gruff and often disagreeable, he loves the children. His main activity is helping in the store.

Themes

American Dream

For Maya Angelou, in *I Know Why the Caged Bird Sings,* the American dream was somewhere over the bridge in the white part of town. Through her keen perception and her probing insight into her character Marguerite Johnson, she sees reality in all its beauty and ugliness. Eventually, Marguerite comes to terms with the fact that she is forever black and that she can succeed in a world filled with prejudice. The best example of this is her persistence in becoming the first black streetcar conductor in San Francisco. She has learned to outwit her tormentors, who include snobby whites, pretentious blacks, and most of the men she encounters along the difficult path of growing up.

Coming of Age

Along the way, Marguerite has many mentors to guide her in *I Know Why the Caged Bird Sings*—her grandmother Annie Henderson, Mrs. Flowers, her mother Vivian Baxter Johnson, and her high-school teacher, Miss Kirwin. All her guides are strong women who have preceded her and have survived the similar trials of youth that she is going through. Angelou's portrayal of black males is quite negative; most of the male characters in the book are the weak links in the chain toward her success.

It thus becomes a feminist manifesto as well as the story of a shy and awkward black child who blossoms into an assured and self-confident young woman. Writes Angelou, 'The fact that the adult American Negro female emerges a formidable character is often met with amazement, distaste and even belligerence. It is seldom accepted as an inevitable outcome of the struggle won by survivors and deserves respect if not enthusiastic acceptance."

Prejudice and Tolerance

Prejudice in I Know Why the Caged Bird Sings takes different forms in the three places where the Johnson children spend their young years. In deep-South Arkansas, lynchings are the ultimate threat to black freedom. In St. Louis, their white-seeming octoroon (one-eighth black) grandmother Baxter has special influence in the political arena of a seamy city. And their mother creates a buoyant and independent life through wit, talent, beauty, and determination. In San Francisco, Marguerite fights the establishment to go where no black has gone before.

Topics for Further Study

- Research the history of the Ku Klux Klan in the 1930s and 1940s and today. Note any changes in the activities of this organization over the years and debate whether or not it is still a danger to U.S. society.

- Compare employment practices and laws in the 1930s and the 1940s with those of today. Emphasize the status of women and minorities.

- Argue whether or not affirmative-action programs have outlived their usefulness. Support your argument with specific examples and current statistics.

Education

Although *I Know Why the Caged Bird Sings* is often referred to as an autobiography, Angelou's use of novelistic techniques make literary study of the work a valuable endeavor.

Throughout *I Know Why the Caged Bird Sings,* Maya Angelou's strong belief in the power of education is evident. It is education, through reading, which brings Marguerite out of her silence after her rape, and education that allows her to create a better life for herself. In the author's own life, it was her love of knowledge and her intelligence that propelled her into multiple and exciting careers.

Style

Point of View

Although *I Know Why the Caged Bird Sings* is often referred to as an autobiography, Angelou's use of novelistic techniques makes literary study of the work a valuable endeavor.

Throughout *I Know Why the Caged Bird Sings,* we see people, places, and events through the imagination of Marguerite. While she often keeps her own counsel, she carries on a private dialogue with herself that is in turn poetic, humorous, sardonic, and tragic. Gifted with the ability to see through shams and affectations, she cuts through to the quick of her observations. She knows intuitively what is real and what is phony, and she processes all this information intellectually over her growing-up years and gradually forms a positive self-image. The shy, awkward child becomes the determined, talented young adult.

Narration

Key to communicating Marguerite's point of view is the narration of the novel. Angelou uses the first person "I" to tell events, giving the reader direct access to Marguerite's thoughts and concerns. Since the narration is limited to what Marguerite chooses to tell, the reader only gets to see events through her perceptions, and can only learn about other characters from Marguerite's descriptions and assumptions. This technique is common in autobiographical works, however, whose intention is to communicate the experiences of one individual.

Setting

The multiple settings in *I Know Why the Caged Bird Sings* in which Marguerite acquires her diversified knowledge of people and culture also highlight the difficulties she has in integrating her experiences into a single philosophy and identity. But by the end of the book the reader feels that she knows who she is and what she wants in life. What the reader can't know is how far she may stray from this identity before she discovers her true self.

Allusion

Throughout the novel Marguerite alludes, or makes reference to, several songs and poems that come to have significance for her. When a group of white children torment Marguerite's grandmother, "Momma" begins singing a series of hymns as a way to turn aside their attempts to humiliate her. These songs, such as "Bread of Heaven," recall the spirituals sung by slaves as a means of dealing with the cruelties of slavery. During Marguerite's eighth-grade graduation, after a white speaker only speaks of limited roles for her and her fellow graduates, she feels bitterness and shame until the valedictorian leads the audience in "Life Ev'ry Voice and Sing," a poem by James Weldon Johnson. Made into a song and considered the "Negro national anthem," this poem helps Marguerite recall the difficult but triumphant struggle her ancestors have been through: "I was no longer simply a member of the proud graduating class of 1940; I was a proud member of the wonderful, beautiful Negro race." And of course, the title of the book makes reference to an inspirational poem by Paul Laurence Dunbar entitled "Sympathy," which recalls themes of freedom and self-discovery.

Conflicts over Civil Rights

Although the action in *I Know Why the Caged Bird Sings* takes place in the early 1930s through the late 1940s, just after World War II had finally ended, the book was published in 1970, at a time of civil unrest and protest in the nation's black communities. The civil rights movement had splintered with the assassination of its chief architect, Dr. Martin Luther King Jr., in April 1968, and protest riots followed. African Americans wavered between following the pacifism that had characterized his leadership and a more outspoken form of protest that had arisen during the last years of King's life. For a time, the latter won out, driven by a climbing black population in many of the nation's major cities. Fueled by outrage over the prejudice, poverty, crime, and unemployment that kept black Americans living in the inner cities—in areas no whites would live—major race riots broke out in Los Angeles, Detroit, Chicago, and New York, among many other cities, resulting in death, injury, and destruction of property. In part, such violence stemmed from a consciousness raised by the Black Power movement, which had gained prominence beginning in 1966. Its tenets overtly pitted blacks against whites. Oakland, California, was home to the Black Panther movement, a group of militant, armed urban youth who advocated the arming of ghetto residents against predatory and racially intolerant police officers. Predictably, these two groups of gun-bearers met head-to-head in a number of violent episodes in California cities. Meanwhile, the Vietnam War preoccupied civil rights workers in King's nonviolence camp. The conflict in southeast Asia was draining valuable financial resources away from the war on poverty within America and also drawing an inordinate number of inner-city youth to their deaths in its faraway jungles.

Compare & Contrast

- **1930s:** Blacks are barred from voting in the South; although this discrimination by race is illegal, states use poll taxes and other laws to restrict voting rights.

  1970: After the Voting Rights Act of 1965 and Civil Rights Act of 1968, racial discrimination is banned from housing, public places, and the voting booth. African Americans begin to successfully run for political office in greater numbers.

  Today: Blacks are entitled to vote all over the United States, many cities in both North and South have black mayors, and many black men and women serve in both the U.S. House and Senate.

- **1930s:** Schools are segregated and unequal, and blacks are blocked from living in white neighborhoods all over the U.S.

  1970: School segregation is illegal, and some courts have even ordered busing to enforce desegregation of schools.

  Today: Enforced desegregation has been successfully challenged in the courts. School segregation and housing discrimination is illegal but persists anyway, as economic factors often split populations into racially divided neighborhoods.

- **1930s:** During the Depression, there are limited job opportunities for African Americans, who face overt prejudice in both the South and North.

  1970: Affirmative Action programs begin to be enacted to offer minorities, including women and blacks, greater access to jobs and education.

  Today: Civil Rights Laws protect the employment rights of blacks and other minorities, although affirmative action programs are themselves being challenged as discriminatory.

- **1930s:** Lynching—a form of

vigilante "justice" in which white mobs torture and murder blacks—often goes unpunished.

1970: Lynching is prosecuted as murder, and is seen less and less, even in the South.

Today: Racial attacks by mobs on individuals are very rare, although individual crimes are often motivated by racial hatred. Race-related violence is often prosecuted as a separate crime.

Black Arts Movement

The written word was a powerful tool in the struggle for African American rights and the creation of a black voice in national affairs. Primarily associated with writer-poet Amiri Baraka (formerly known, when he was a Beat poet, as LeRoi Jones), the black arts movement included members who espoused the philosophy that for black artists to indulge in empty avant-gardism or to create art that was grounded in the personal rather than the political was folly. These members of the black arts movement held that black artists, unlike their middle-class white counterparts, did not have the luxury of refusing to politicize their work. Some young mavericks of the movement openly criticized fore-runners like Paul Laurence Dunbar, Jean Toomer, and Langston Hughes, as well as the

Harlem Renaissance as a whole, for a presumed lack of social consciousness. Angelou's book came out in striking contrast to the black arts movement since her own personal experience never takes a back seat to the problems of society. However, *I Know Why the Caged Bird Sings* is directed at other blacks, even though Angelou was well aware that a white audience would read it too. This idea of the black arts movement—that black writers must stop protesting to whites and start educating blacks—is one with which Angelou's autobiography is in accord.

The not-so-new South

In the late 1960s, civil rights activists were still struggling to achieve equality in many arenas, just as they had throughout the years Angelou depicts in *Caged Bird*. After the Civil War, hopes ran high among black Americans that their social, political, and economic lot in life would markedly improve. However, white Southerners employed strategies that dashed these hopes and halted the strides made toward civil rights following the war. In response to the Fifteenth Amendment to the U.S. Constitution, which guaranteed that the right of citizens to vote would not be denied by any state on account of race, Southern states quickly moved to exclude black voters on other, nonracial grounds—for example, an inability to read or to pay a poll tax. Similarly, they passed laws to establish a policy of segregation in society at large.

States could legally force black citizens to live in separate neighborhoods and to use separate telephone booths, restrooms, drinking fountains, cemeteries—and even different Bibles on which to swear in the courtroom. This social situation prevails in Stamps, Arkansas, where Angelou grows up and where a strict color line, marked by the railroad tracks, divides the black from the white parts of town.

Elsewhere in the United States the situation began to change by the mid-1940s, the period in which the autobiography ends. In *Hansberry v. Lee* (1940) the Supreme Court ruled that blacks could not be restricted from purchasing homes in white neighborhoods. And in *Morgan v. Commonwealth of Virginia* (1946) the Court ruled that segregation in interstate bus travel was unconstitutional. Yet there was also violent resistance to such change. A riot broke out, for example, after black welders were assigned to work along with white welders in an Alabama shipyard, and white supremacist groups such as the Ku Klux Klan dedicated themselves to "punishing" blacks for standing up for their rights. They were responsible for many mob killings, known as lynchings; in the 1940s the number of blacks lynched in Arkansas alone since the 1880s had exceeded 200. The practice would not die out completely until the late 1960s and remained a very real threat during the period that Angelou recounts in her autobiography.

Ongoing migration

In the early part of the century, many blacks in the South had to scratch out a living by hiring themselves out to the white landowners as cotton-pickers. As agriculture became more mechanized, this meager source of income dried up. Many black families migrated to northern cities, in hopes of finding jobs in the North's booming industries. The passing of nativist immigration laws in the 1920s provided added impetus to Southern blacks in their northward migration. These new restrictions meant the virtual closing of U.S. borders to the working-class southern and eastern Europeans who had previously made up a large portion of the factory labor force in cities such as New York and Detroit. The void soon became filled by black Americans willing to relocate hundreds of miles for the chance to become industrial workers outside the South. The decades in which *Caged Bird* takes place saw 458,000 blacks leaving the South in the 1930s and 1,345,400 in the 1940s. However, many were also disappointed to find that the North was no cure for racism against blacks. Prejudice just wore a different face.

Prohibition-Era St. Louis

The young characters in *I Know Why the Caged Bird Sings* are in St. Louis during the era of Prohibition (1920-33), when the manufacture and sale of alcohol was outlawed in the United States. During the time of Prohibition, speakeasies and gambling dens became the gathering places of drinkers, gamblers, and pleasure-seekers. Maya's mother undoubtedly was involved in illegal activities in the casinos where she worked. But Prohibition badly damaged U.S. society when the mob moved in and took over the liquor industry. Therefore, it is hard to criticize Maya's mother for breaking a bad law, especially since she was trying to support a family. Prohibition was repealed in 1933, although every Southern state continued to place certain restrictions on liquor—perhaps because of the influence of conservative Christian churches, which traditionally disdained alcohol. In contrast, Northern states abandoned most legislative controls.

Critical Overview

Published in 1970, *I Know Why the Caged Bird Sings* won critical acclaim and was nominated for the National Book Award. Wrote critic Sidonie Ann Smith in *Southern Humanities Review,* "Angelou's genius as a writer is her ability to recapture the texture of the way of life in the texture of its idioms, its idiosyncratic vocabulary and especially in its process of image-making." This book, the first of five in a series describing her life and her continuing search for self-realization, was the best received of the collection. Some posit that the reason is that in her subsequent autobiographical novels, Angelou—who went through many ups and downs in her life—was a less appealing character, though her lifelong achievements thus far seem to belie such criticism.

Critical analysis of Angelou's autobiographical prose has mainly focused on *Caged Bird* and its portrayal of a black woman's coming of age. Assessing the work within the tradition of African American memoirs, George Kent notes in *African American Autobiography: A Collection of Critical Essays* that the work stands out in its use of the imagination: "*I Know Why* creates a unique place within black autobiographical tradition .... by its special stance toward the self, the community, and the universe, and by a form exploiting the full measure of imagination necessary to acknowledge both beauty and absurdity." Other critics have examined the manner in which Angelou's characters survive in a hostile world. Myra K. McMurry, for instance, observes in *South Atlantic Bulletin* how Momma serves as a role model for Marguerite, and indeed for all people fighting racism: "She triumphs not only in spite of her restrictions, but because of them. It is because, as a Black woman, she must maintain the role of respect toward the white children that she discovers another vehicle for her true emotions. She has used her cage creatively to transcend it." Suzette A. Henke suggests in *Traditions, Voices, and Dreams* that this autobiographical work, in presenting a voice that is not often heard, "has the potential to be .... a revolutionary form of writing." In the "comic and triumphant" end of the novel, writes Henke, Marguerite's "victory suggests an implicit triumph over the white bourgeoisie [middle class], whose values have flagrantly been subverted."

While the work has been praised, analyzed, and taught in classrooms, it has also met with censorship. The graphic portrayal of Marguerite's rape as well as the acceptance of her teenage, out-of-wedlock pregnancy have inspired the most challenges. However, Opal Moore suggests that these events offer students a chance to examine important issues. As she writes in *Censored Books: Critical Viewpoints:* "With the appropriate effort, this literary experience can assist readers of any racial or economic group in meeting their own, often unarticulated doubts, questions, fears, and perhaps assist in their own search for dignity."

Sources

Suzette A. Henke, "Women's Life-Writing and the Minority Voice: Maya Angelou, Maxine Hong Kingston, and Alice Walker," in *Traditions, Voices, and Dreams: The American Novel since the 1960s,* edited by Melvin J. Friedman and Ben Siegel, University of Delaware Press, 1995, pp. 210-33.

George Kent, "Maya Angelou's 'I Know Why the Caged Bird Sings' and Black Autobiographical Tradition," in *African American Autobiography: A Collection of Critical Essays,* Prentice-Hall, 1993, pp. 162-70.

Myra K. McMurry, "Role-Playing as Art in Maya Angelou's *Caged Bird,*" in *South Atlantic Bulletin,* No. 2, May, 1976, pp. 106-11.

Opal Moore, "Learning to Live: When the Bird Breaks from the Cage," in *Censored Books: Critical Viewpoints,* Nicholas J. Karolides, Lee Burress, John M. Kean, eds., 1993, pp. 306-16.

Sidonie Ann Smith, "The Song of a Caged Bird: Maya Angelou's Quest after Self-Acceptance," in *The Southern Humanities Review,* Fall, 1973, pp. 365-75.

For Further Study

James Bertolino, "Maya Angelou Is Three Writers: I Know Why the Caged Bird Sings," in *Censored Books: Critical Viewpoints,* edited by N. J. Karolides, L. Burgess, and J. M. Kean, The Scarecrow Press, 1993, pp. 299-305.

> Bertolino views Angelou as a gifted shaper of words and literary devices, an intensely honest person, and an important social commentator.

Jeffrey M. Elliot, editor, *Conversations with Maya Angelou,* University of Mississippi Press, 1989.

> An insightful collection of reprinted interviews with Angelou.

Onita Estes-Hicks, "The Way We Were: Precious Memories of the Black Segregated South," in *African American Review,Vol.* 27, No. 1, pp. 9-18.

> Estes-Hicks places Angelou's autobiography within the tradition of Black Southern autobiographies by comparing and contrasting with other writers.

Mary Jane Lupton, "Singing the Black Mother: Maya Angelou and Autobiographical Continuity," in *Black American Literature Forum,Vol.* 24, No. 2, Summer 1990, pp. 257-76.

> Discusses the unifying theme of

motherhood in Angelou's autobiographies.

Carol E. Neubauer, "Maya Angelou: Self and a Song of Freedom in the Southern Tradition," in *Southern Women Writers: The New Generation,* edited by T. Bond Inge, The University of Alabama Press, 1990, pp. 114-42.

Summarizes Angelou's career and discusses recurring themes in her poetry, including "Caged Bird."

Sondra O'Neale, "Reconstruction of the Composite Self: New Images of Black Women in Maya Angelou's Continuing Autobiography," in *Black Women Writers (1950-1980): A Critical Evaluation,* edited by M. Evans, Anchor Press/Doubleday, 1984, pp. 25-37.

O'Neale discusses Angelou's racial identification and how she subverts stereotypical ideas of the Black Woman.

Mary Vermillion, "Reembodying the Self: Representations of Rape in 'Incidents in the Life of a Slave Girl' and 'I Know Why the Caged Bird Sings'," in *Biography,* Vol. 15, No. 3, Summer, 1992, pp. 243-60.

Vermillion gives a sensitive and perceptive discussion of the rape and its connection to a larger theme of oppression in the autobiography.

Pierre A. Walker, "Racial Protest, Identity, Words,

and Form in Maya Angelou's 'I Know Why the Caged Bird Sings'," in *College Literature,* Vol. 222, Oct. 1995, pp. 91-108.

> Walker focuses on the literary qualities to assert the autobiography traces the steps of the author's political self from racial helplessness to active protest.

Lightning Source UK Ltd.
Milton Keynes UK
UKHW020030110123
415109UK00015B/1039